"BLOOD AND GUTS"

"BLOOD AND GUTS"

The True Story of Gen. George S. Patton, USA

JOHN DEVANEY

Illustrated with photographs

Julian Messner New York

Copyright © 1982 by John Devaney

All rights reserved including the right of
reproduction in whole or in part in any form.
Published by Julian Messner, a Simon & Schuster
Division of Gulf & Western Corporation.
Simon & Schuster Building,
1230 Avenue of the Americas,
New York, New York 10020.

JULIAN MESSNER and colophon are trademarks of
Simon & Schuster

Manufactured in the United States of America
Designed by A Good Thing Inc.

Library of Congress Cataloging in Publication Data

Devaney, John.
  "Blood and guts".

  Bibliography: p.
  Includes index.
  Summary: A biography of the controversial
commander of the Third Army in World War II.
  1. Patton, George S. (George Smith), 1885–1945
—Juvenile literature. 2. United States—History,
Military—20th century—Juvenile literature.
3. United States. Army—Biography—Juvenile litera-
ture. 4. Generals—United States—Biography—
Juvenile literature. [1. Patton, George S. (George
Smith), 1885–1945. 2. Generals] I. Title.
E745.P3D48 1982   940.54'1'0924 [B] [92]   82-60636

ISBN 0-671-44273-2

For My Father
  Who Also Served in the AEF

MESSNER BOOKS BY JOHN DEVANEY

"Blood and Guts":
The True Story of Gen. George S. Patton, USA

The Picture Story of Terry Bradshaw

Photographs courtesy U.S. Dept of Defense

Maps by Barbara Devaney

CONTENTS

"Attack!"

Ike stared at the faces of his generals. Outside the windows of the stone headquarters building in France, a winter storm howled.

A few days earlier, 200,000 German troops had charged through the Ardennes Forest in nearby Belgium, surprising 80,000 American soldiers. Thousands of Americans were killed, their blood-soaked bodies strewn over the snowy hills of the Ardennes.

Like an iron dagger, German tanks were striking toward the English Channel. If the Germans reached the Channel, Ike's Allied army would be cut in half. Hundreds of thousands of American, British, Canadian, and French soldiers would be captured or slaughtered, and Adolf Hitler's Nazi army might yet win World War II.

General of the Army Dwight D. Eisenhower, called "Ike," was the Supreme Commander of the Allied army. On this morning of December 19, 1944, Ike had assembled his top generals to find a way to stop the German charge to the sea.

Several generals offered plans. Ike frowned. He didn't think any of the plans would work. There was silence. Then Ike turned to Lieutenant General George S. Patton, known to his Third Army troops as "Old Blood and Guts."

"When can you attack?" Ike asked Patton.

Patton's rosy-cheeked, brick-jawed face was thoughtful for several moments. He smoothed his grey, close-cropped hair. Then his piercing voice cut across the room. "On December 22," he said, "with three divisions."

A murmur of surprise rumbled around the table. Generals stared at one another. Today was already December 19. How could Patton attack in only three days? His Third Army tanks and troops were a hundred miles from the Ardennes. And between them and the Ardennes was a fierce blizzard, icy roads, and drifting banks of snow. Attack in three days? Impossible!

"Some people seemed surprised," Patton wrote in his diary that night. "However, I believe it can be done."

Ike had doubts, too. Three divisions, he told Patton at the meeting, were not enough to halt the German charge.

"I can beat the Germans with three divisions," Patton said in a firm voice. "If we wait to get more divisions, we lose surprise."

Ike approved Patton's plan. It seemed the only one likely

Third Army troops place wood on a road near Bastogne so their tanks won't skid on the ice.

to succeed. Patton rose, the three silver stars of a lieutenant general glittering on his shoulders. He strode from the room.

Minutes later he was on the telephone barking orders to his staff at Third Amy headquarters. Within a few hours, Third Army riflemen were climbing into the backs of trucks. Drivers slipped into their 30-ton Grant tanks. Engines coughed and roared alive, belching black smoke into the frosty air.

That night a column of Third Army tanks and trucks struggled northward through the blizzard. Yellow head-light beams swung wildly in the blackness as trucks and tanks skidded on the icy roads. In the open backs of the trucks, numbed riflemen huddled together as wind and snow whipped their faces. And they wondered: Where was Blood and Guts sending them now?

They found out at dawn on December 22. As Patton had promised, his three divisions attacked the Germans. Riflemen and machine gunners dashed over the twisting, snow-covered trails. Tanks plunged through deep gullies, German bullets spattering off their flanks. American guns rained shells that blew away German tanks and scattered German troops.

From headquarters Patton radioed orders for a drive toward the town of Bastogne. American paratroopers were holding the town, encircled by German artillery, tanks, and machine gunners. The paratroopers' ammunition was dwindling fast. In a day or two there would be none, and the GIs would have to surrender the town.

The Germans needed Bastogne to keep open a supply line of fuel to their tanks. Americans could block that fuel line by holding the town. Then the German drive to the sea would sputter out and stop.

Patton confers with Brig. General Anthony McAuliffe,
Bastogne's commander, who told Germans
demanding his surrender: "Nuts!"

Patton paced the floor. He wished he were there at Bastogne, firing a gun. He always wanted to be in the midst of the fighting. As a colonel in World War I, he had walked behind his tanks during a charge at German machine guns. A bullet had cut him down. Now, 25 years later, the thunder and lightning of combat still drew him like a magnet toward the front.

Patton called for his Jeep and drove north toward the Ardennes, siren wailing. The flame-red flag with the three white stars of a lieutenant general whipped in the wind. Patton stood erect in the Jeep, his helmet gleaming in the pale sunlight, his hard-muscled 6-foot-1, 190-pound body taking a jolting. His billowy riding pants were tucked into gleaming, silver-spurred boots. At his side was strapped an ivory-handled Colt .45 pistol. He was an heroic figure.

Patton's Jeep roared by a line of trucks carrying 90th Division soldiers toward the fighting. The men stood and cheered as Patton came by. He turned to them and waved.

"It is good for morale," Patton once said, "for soldiers to see their general going with them toward the front."

And that night, remembering the applause he had received from men he was sending toward death, he wrote, "It was the most moving moment of my life."

The next day, back at headquarters, he scanned a message. It was from a tank commander who had been halted by shellfire on the edge of Bastogne. The commander wanted to try to dash through the shellfire and enter the town. This was risky. Even if a few tanks were able to enter Bastogne, the German circle could close behind them. The tanks would then be trapped inside the town.

But Patton liked this kind of bold idea. "Attack . . . and attack fast," he told his commanders. "Always move forward, always attack. The longer that your men are under fire, the more of your men will be killed. End a battle quickly and you save lives."

"Try it," Patton radioed the tank commander.

The Third Army tanks broke through the German circle and clanked into Bastogne's shell-smashed streets. Then the tank commander lined up the tanks so they formed a pipeline of steel from Bastogne to the American tanks outside the town. The tanks kept blasting at the Germans, holding them back as fresh American troops dashed through the pipeline into Bastogne. They carried food and ammunition and were greeted with cheers by the cold, hungry, exhausted paratroopers.

Patton, meanwhile, had moved most of his Third Army into the Ardennes—nearly a quarter of a million troops. They hammered at the sides of the German column that had stabbed so deeply into the American line. The German tanks and troops were forced to stop their advance toward the Channel. The tanks were out of gas and the troops were toppling amid a hail of bullets and shells. Hilter's army turned back and began its final retreat toward Germany and surrender.

Patton's Third Army had turned defeat into victory. Eisenhower later wrote that Patton's Third Army "moved farther and faster and engaged more divisions than any other Army in the history of the United States."

"Old Blood and Guts" had won again. In two world wars, Patton had never been beaten in battle. And he enjoyed war. As an 18-year-old cadet at West Point, he

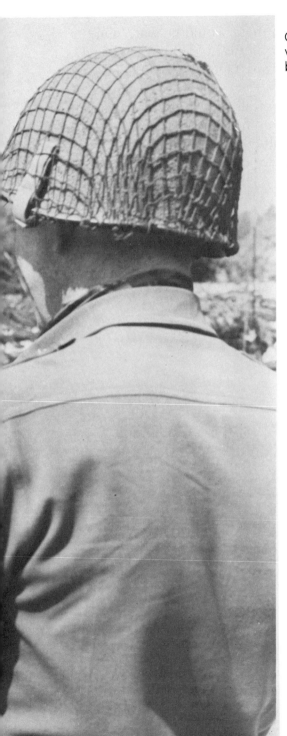

Old Blood and Guts in victory: he never lost a battle.

wrote to his father, "I wish there would be war." On the eve of World War II, he wrote to his old pal Dwight D. Eisenhower, "Hoping we are together for a long and *bloody* war."

Yet, as a youth, he was afraid that he was a coward. "That old 'fear of fear,' " as he called his inner dread, haunted him for the first half of his life, until he found out he was not a coward at a place called Cheppy in France in World War I.

. . . A Coward?

He had run! Like a dirty coward, he had run away from a fight. Another boy had challenged him to a fist fight. And he had fled, his heart pounding.

Alone in his room, the 14-year-old Georgie, as his parents called him, wondered if he should tell his father he had turned tail? He, George Patton, the grandson of a war hero—was he a coward?

George spoke to his father. His voice catching, he repeated his question aloud: Was he a coward?

No, his father told him. No member of the Patton family could be a coward. Like his fighting ancestors, George had "good" blood. The Pattons had fought under the flags of Scottish princes and English kings. After the Pattons moved to America, one had fought in the Revolutionary

War under George Washington. And another, George's grandfather, had died on a Civil War battlefield.

His father said to George, "While ages of gentility might make a man of your breeding reluctant to engage in a fist fight, that same breeding might make him perfectly willing to face death from weapons with a smile."

A Patton might not be a street brawler, his father was saying. But a Patton would always be a brave soldier, willing to die for his country.

The whip-slim, blond-haired George nodded. But his father's words had not made George's doubts disappear. He wrote about those doubts in his diary, once accusing himself of having "a weak and cowardly nature." Patton kept a diary all his life and in the diary he put his innermost secrets.

Patton felt he did not look fierce enough. Often he stood in front of the mirror and tried to put a menacing look on his face. He did that for most of his life, seeking what he called "the ideal fighting face." He never found it.

George was born on November 11, 1885 and grew up on a ranch near Pasadena, California. His father, George Smith Patton, was a successful lawyer whose own father had been killed in the Civil War. George's father had moved to California from the family's war-torn home in Virginia. But George Smith Patton was still the Virginia gentleman. He was proud of his family's history.

At night he read stories to his son Georgie about warrior princes and kings. George was fascinated and began to idolize warriors like Alexander the Great and King Arthur and his Knights of the Round Table. He daydreamed about battles. And he idolized General Robert E. Lee, the

Virginian who had led the Confederate army in the Civil War.

When George was eleven, his father gave him a glittering French army sabre. Gripping the sabre, George went around the ranch on his horse. He slashed at the tops of cactus bushes. He pretended he was cutting off the heads of his enemies. The sabre held high, he dreamed that he was Lieutenant General Robert E. Lee, and an army of soldiers followed him.

Each summer the Patton family went to Catalina Island, which was off the California coast. There the athletic George swam and fished. One summer, when George was seventeen, the Patton family became friendly with a family from Massachusetts. The family's name was Ayer, and one of the daughters, Beatrice, took George's breath away.

George told Beatrice of his ambition to be a conquering military hero like Alexander the Great and a leader of men like Robert E. Lee. At summer's end Beatrice and George promised to write to each other—a promise they kept for more than 40 years.

That fall of 1903 George entered the Virginia Military Institute. George's father and grandfather had also marched across the VMI parade ground as cadets. He wanted to follow their footsteps. If he graduated from VMI, he could become a lieutenant in the United States Army and one day, maybe, a general.

"It is in war alone that I am fitted to do anything of importance," he wrote to Beatrice. He had dreamed so long of war and battles, he told her, "that they seem real and everything else unreal."

He told his father how he wanted to be as great as Alexander or Robert E. Lee. "I would be willing to live in torture and die tomorrow," he said, "if for one day I could really be great."

Patton was not a good student. In spelling drills he mangled words. In math class he stared, dazed, at the long row of numbers the instructor put on the blackboard. Midway through his first year, Patton was failing in math and English. As hard as life was in the classroom, it was even harder outside away from books. As a first-year student he was called a Rat. Rats were hounded by the older cadets. They had to stand at attention as cadets screamed insults into their faces. Rats had to obey humiliating orders like shouting, "I am dumb, sir, I am dumb!"

Patton endured every ordeal. He would do anything, he told Beatrice, to be an officer.

He desperately wanted to go to the U.S. Military Academy at West Point. A West Point graduate had a much better chance of becoming a general than a VMI graduate. But Patton feared that his math and English were not good enough for him to be appointed to West Point.

His father, meanwhile, had become the district attorney of Los Angeles and knew many influential men. He asked one of those men, a congressman, to appoint George to West Point. In the spring of 1904, George talked to the congressman, who said later, "He certainly has a soldier's look and walk!" He appointed Patton to West Point. That summer Patton walked through the gates of West Point, high above the Hudson River in New York State.

He faced another year of humiliations.

Like a Rat at VMI, a first-year cadet at West Point had to obey every order of upperclass cadets. Upperclassmen shouted at the Plebes, "Chest *in,* chin *up, straighten* those shoulders!" Patton and other Plebes marched for hours in 100-degree heat, then were forced to leap into ice-cold baths. "If war is hell," Patton wrote to Beatrice during his first year at West Point, "West Point is war."

Math was still impossibly hard for Patton and at the end of that Plebe year, he failed the course. He must go through another year as a Plebe or be dismissed. For the *third* year in a row, he would be under the heel of upperclassmen. Patton told Beatrice and his father, "I'll do it . . . it is as natural for me to be a soldier as it is to breathe, and as hard to give up as breathing."

Repeating his Plebe year, Patton finally passed math. In most other courses he was given grades barely above the passing level. But as an athlete he was one of West Point's best. He set a school record as a hurdler. He was one of the academy's flashiest swordsmen. He smacked in goals for the polo team. "He is a madman on horseback," one polo player said after a match. He played football with the same wild abandon. He broke so many bones in practice that he was never sound enough to play in a game.

On the parade ground Cadet George S. Patton strutted smartly. His shrill voice rang out commands. Cadets under his command marched with a precision that raised the eyebrows of majors and colonels. In his senior year Patton was appointed adjutant of the Corps of Cadets, the second-highest rank that any cadet could attain. And in June, 1909, as his proud father and mother and Beatrice watched, he strode up to the platform and received his diploma. His mother and Beatrice pinned on his shoulders the gold bars of a second lieutenant in the United States Army. George chose to serve with the horse soldiers in the cavalry because "cavalry officers get to be generals sooner than foot soldiers."

Several months later, George and Beatrice were married. The Pattons went to live at Fort Sheridan near Chicago, where he commanded a troop of cavalry soldiers. During the next few years, George won many medals as one of the Army's top marksmen with a pistol. With a sabre he rarely lost a match. His skills were so great that he represented the United States in the pentathlon at the 1912 Olympic Games.

Patton's soldiers were astonished by his boldness on horseback. Once, as he tried to tame a horse, the horse's head snapped back and struck his face. Blood gushed from the wound, but Patton stayed in the saddle of the bucking horse until it was quiet. A doctor patched up his torn face. "I wish I had your nerve," the doctor said to him. Patton smiled. Later, however, he wrote in his diary that he wondered if he stayed on the horse out of courage or to hide that "weak and cowardly nature."

In 1916, he and Beatrice were stationed at dusty Fort Bliss, near El Paso, on the Texas–Mexican border. Gunfighters walked the streets of El Paso. Patton became a friend of Dave Allison, the El Paso sheriff and a former gunfighter. Allison told Patton how to gun down a fleeing bandit, "Always shoot at his horse."

That spring of 1916, a band of Mexicans crossed the

Lt. Patton in Mexico with Pershing—on Patton's right hip, the gun that shot Cardenas.

border and charged into a small town, Columbus, in New Mexico, their guns blazing. They left behind the bullet-torn bodies of 17 Americans. The enraged President of the

United States, Woodrow Wilson, ordered the army to invade Mexico and capture or kill the Mexican leader, Pancho Villa.

The commander of the American army was General John Pershing, a tough and feisty leader who was called "Black Jack" by his men. Pershing organized his army at Fort Bliss, Texas.

Patton was told that his unit would not be riding into Mexico with Pershing. Others would go to war. George Patton would sit at home. That war he had always wanted . . . so near to him, yet so far. He told himself he would find a way to go with Pershing.

For several days he waited near the general's house, hoping to meet him. Finally, one afternoon he saw Pershing. The lieutenant rushed up to the general, saluted, and begged to go to Mexico.

"Why?" growled Black Jack.

"Because I want to go more than anyone else."

Pershing snorted and walked away. But Patton's boldness had impressed him. A few days later Patton got orders. He would ride into Mexico next to Pershing as one of the general's aides.

At last, at the age of 30, war had come to George Patton, not the war of his books and daydreams, but a real blood-and-guts kind of war.

Gunfight at the
Rubio Ranch

Patton ran toward the gate of the main house of the Rubio Ranch, a rifle gripped in his left hand, a pistol at his hip. Behind him ran an American scout. The other ten soldiers in Patton's party had jumped out of their automobiles and were racing to surround the house. One of Pancho Villa's captains, Julio Cardenas, was hiding there.

As Patton ran toward the arched main gate of the house, he heard the sound of hoof beats. Three men on horses charged out of the gate. Patton whipped out his pistol and shouted, "Stop!" The horsemen rode straight at Patton, firing their guns. Bullets whizzed by his head. One kicked up gravel that sprayed his boots. Patton stood his ground, and coolly fired his pistol—once, again, then three more times in rapid succession. A horse was hit, but did not stop. Another bullet broke the arm of one of the riders—Cardenas.

The shower of bullets from Patton and the other Americans stopped the charging horsemen. They wheeled and dashed back through the gate.

Patton ran to the side of the house and reloaded his pistol. Three enemy bullets hit a foot above his head, spraying Patton with chips of clay.

Patton ducked around the corner of the house. He saw a single horseman galloping toward the gate. Patton recalled the advice of the old gunfighter: he fired at the fleeing man's horse. The horse stumbled and fell, pinning the rider for a few moments. The man pulled free, rose, and fired at the Americans. Patton and the others returned the fire, riddling the man with bullets. He was dead before his body touched the ground.

An American shouted that another man was trying to escape from the house.

The fleeing man was Cardenas. He ran along the top of a wall. One of the soldiers aimed his rifle and fired. Cardenas toppled to the ground. But he jumped up, a gun in his hand, and fired at the rifleman. He missed. The rifleman fired again and Cardenas fell dead.

Patton wrote to Beatrice, telling of his first battle. "I have always expected to be scared," he wrote, "but was not, nor was I excited . . . I never heard a bullet but some say you do not at such close range. I wondered (why) I was not hit, they were so close."

Newspapermen riding with the American army wrote excitedly of the battle. A headline in the *New York Times* of May 23, 1916 told of "Lieut. Patton and Ten Men" killing the 'Mexican bandits.' " Another newspaper reporter wrote that the battle at the Rubio Ranch was "one of the prettiest fights of the campaign," which up to then had been dull.

Pershing's army chased Pancho Villa but could not capture him, and in 1917 the army returned to the United States. Black Jack and his soldiers were needed for bigger and bloodier battles. World War I was raging in Europe. The United States was poised to plunge into that inferno of death and destruction. And George Patton was soon to meet a terrifying new weapon that he would ride to fame.

"War!"

"You are the first American tanks. You must establish the fact that *American tanks never surrender.* . . . As long as one tank is able to move, it must go FORWARD."

Those orders were delivered by Lieutenant Colonel George S. Patton to the men of his first and second Light Tank Battalions. They were the first Americans to fight in tanks.

The tank had been developed in 1914 by a British officer. The tanks crawled forward on their caterpillar treads. Bullets and shells bounced off their sides of steel. The 10-ton monsters plowed through fences of barbed wire, opening the way for foot soldiers who crouched behind the tanks. The tanks were the first wave in an attack. They squashed soldiers cowering in shell holes. By the summer of 1918 the tank had become the terror of World War I, feared by soldiers on both sides.

Patton had arrived in France in 1917, still an aide to General Pershing. He was among the first members of the American Expeditionary Force (AEF) to land in France to fight with their British and French allies against the Germans.

Patton was fascinated by the tank. He sensed that the tank would replace the horse as the cavalry of the future. At Patton's request, Pershing transferred him to the new

Lt. Colonel Patton turns to observe the training of his men.

Tank Service. Patton told his officers, "Remember that you are to make paths in the barbed wire and put out machine guns for the infantry. Hence, never get more than a hundred and fifty yards ahead of the infantry. . . . If I find any officer behind the infantry, I will shoot him."

In letters to his wife, he tried to convince her he was safer in a tank than in the trenches. "You either get blown to bits by a direct hit," he wrote cheerfully, "or you are not touched."

But now, as he waited to send his tanks into battle, Patton wondered if he would be brave or turn coward. "There is that old fear of mine," he wrote in his diary, "that fear of fear."

At dawn on the morning of September 12, 1918, Patton watched his tanks waddle down a hill and vanish into a rain squall. As commander of the tanks, Patton had strict orders from his commanding general, "Stay at your command post and phone your report of the battle to me."

But Patton itched to jump into the battle. After half an hour he could not stay away from the fight any longer. He left the command post and followed the tank tracks. He was armed with a pistol and a walking stick. Walking with him were six armed soldiers.

Shells burst around them. Hunks of iron fragments whizzed by their heads. When they heard the whine of an approaching shell, Patton and the soldiers dived to the ground, gripping their steel helmets. But after a few dives, Patton stood erect, walking forward, while his men hugged the heaving ground. "It is futile," he later wrote, "to dodge your fate on the battlefield. The shell that hits you is the one you don't hear."

But he had another reason for walking tall while others cowered—his pride. "The feeling, foolish probably, of being admired by the men lying down is a great stimulus," he wrote to his wife. "It proves that vanity can overcome fear."

Patton saw a tank stalled in a ditch. He shouted to the crew, telling them how to haul the tank out. He started forward again and was only 20 feet from the tank when it was hit by a shell that killed all the men around it.

He caught up with five tanks stalled at a bridge. The crews told him that the bridge was mined and would explode as the tanks crossed.

Patton scanned the bridge with his binoculars. "It isn't mined," he said. "Come on." He walked across the bridge. The tanks clanked after him. Patton's face was serene but his stomach churned. He later said he had expected "to be blown to heaven any moment."

He walked alongside the tanks into a smoking, shattered village. A German soldier rushed out of a building. Patton pointed his pistol and the soldier threw up his hands, surrendering.

Patton met Brigadier General Douglas MacArthur. Patton asked MacArthur, "Can I attack the next town with my tanks?"

"Sure," replied MacArthur, who would become as famous as Patton in World War II.

On the way to the town, however, four of the five tanks chugged to a stop. Their gas tanks were empty. Patton and a lone tank approached the town. They met American soldiers who told Patton they had been stopped by German gunfire from inside the town. Patton told the driver

Patton and one of his French-made tanks.

to lead the men into the town. He stayed on the tank, his legs dangling over the side. The tank rumbled into the town, its treads thundering on the stone streets, its machine gun spitting bullets. Clinging to the tank and waving his pistol, Patton shouted orders. The Americans rounded up 30 German prisoners.

The tank rolled through to the other side of the town. Patton looked down and saw chips of paint flying off the tank. It was being raked by machine-gun bullets that were hitting within inches of his dangling legs. Patton jumped off and dived into a shell hole. "Here," he later confessed in his diary, "I was nervous."

Patton realized he was alone in his shell hole, the tank charging toward the enemy, the other American soldiers a quarter of a mile behind him. Patton realized the lone tank would eventually be stopped by the bullets and the crew captured or killed.

Patton slipped out of the hole and ran after the tank, bullets stitching the ground around him. Panting, he caught up with the tank and rapped on the door with his stick. The driver opened the door, saluted, and said, "What do you want now, Colonel?"

Patton told the driver to turn back. As the tank turned, Patton kept its steel between himself and the whizzing German bullets and got back to the American lines safely.

Patton's "Treat 'em Rough Boys," as the tank fighters called themselves, had led a charge deep into the German lines. More than 6,000 prisoners had been taken. Seven American tanks had been destroyed, but fewer than a dozen of Patton's men had been killed or wounded.

Patton was awarded a Silver Star for riding into battle with the tanks. And he got more of what he hungered for: fame. American newspapers printed stories about him on their front pages under the headline: "Californian Perched on Tank During Battle."

He was also reprimanded by his superior for leaving the command post. "Commanding officers," snapped the general, "should command, not fight."

In his diary Patton shrugged off his general's reprimand. "I will not sit in my dugout and have my men out in the fighting," he wrote. He was delighted by his adventure. Now, he thought, he had chased away his childhood fears of cowardice. In his diary he wrote:

"I at least proved to my own satisfaction that I have nerve."

A Walk Into the
Wall of Death

A week after that American victory, Patton's "Treat 'em Rough Boys" rolled their tanks toward a new front. At dawn on September 26, 1918, Patton stood on a small hill and watched his tanks disappear into a rolling fog. They clanked toward No Man's Land, that shell-torn place between the opposing trenches where men died suddenly and violently.

Patton had promised his commanding general that he would stay in his command post for at least one hour after the tanks attacked. But the roar of war drew him again. With a band of about a dozen soldiers, he followed the trail of the tanks, armed only with the gun that had shot Cardenas and his walking stick.

Shells exploded around them, shaking the muddy ground. They heard the rapid chatter of machine guns and saw bullets tear up the dirt in front of them. Patton ordered his men to take cover in a V-shaped gully.

American soldiers were running by the gully, fleeing from the German shells. Patton ordered them to join his group. Soon a hundred men huddled around him, their eyes wide with fright as shells burst closer. Patton ordered the men to crawl with him to the slope of a nearby hill. They inched close to the top of the slope. The shells, looping over the top of the hill, now fell behind them onto the lower part of the slope.

Patton saw several of his tanks at the bottom of the hill. He sent down his orderly, Private Joe Angelo, with orders for the tanks to climb to the top of the hill so they could attack. But the tanks were mired in a ditch and could not move.

Patton angrily stormed down the hill. Shells were exploding around the tanks. The crews leaped into the ditch. Several men were hit by fragments, blood gushing from gaping wounds in their chests, legs, and arms.

Patton stood at the top of the ditch, ignoring the bursting shells, roaring orders to the huddled men. As Patton shouted at them above the roar of the shellfire, the soldiers began to dig an incline so the tanks could climb out of the ditch. One man tried to crawl back into the ditch. Patton struck him with a shovel. A man was hit by a huge slice of shell fragment and toppled into the ditch, dead. The other men bent low as they dug. Patton strode among them, as straight as a flagpole, shouting, "To hell with them! They can't hit me!"

Finally the tanks lurched out of the ditch. They rumbled up the hill. Patton ran ahead of the tanks and ordered the soldiers pinned on the slope to follow the tanks over the top of the hill. He waved his stick and bellowed, "Let's go get them! Who's with me?"

The soldiers were swept up by the colonel's war cry. They gripped their rifles and followed Patton and the tanks over the crest of the hill.

They walked into a wall of machine-gun bullets. Several men fell. Patton and the others hit the ground.

Patton, his face in the mud, trembled with fear. He was sure he would be blown apart by the streams of bullets that whizzed above his head. He thought of his ancestors who had died on other battlefields. Suddenly he stopped trembling.

"I became calm at once," he later said. He raised his head and screamed, "It is time for another Patton to die!"

He stood up and shouted to the men flat on the ground behind him, "Let's go! Let's go!"

Only six other soldiers jumped up and followed the colonel. One was Private Joe Angelo. The seven walked only a few yards when Angelo turned to see several men fall, then another, and another.

"We are alone!" Angelo shouted above the roar of the gunfire and the screams of the dying.

"Come on anyway!" Patton yelled back. By now he and Angelo were so close to the machine guns that they could see the red glow of the muzzles as they spit their fire.

Patton strode toward the guns, which were firing from behind bushes near a village called Cheppy. Suddenly he slowed, then stumbled drunkenly for several yards. He pitched forward onto the ground.

"Oh God!" Angelo shouted, running to him. "The Colonel's hit and there's no one left!"

Angelo dragged Patton into a shallow shell hole as bullets hummed like furious insects around his ears. He tore open Patton's trousers and saw a blood-filled hole the size of a teacup in Patton's hip. The machine-gun slug had smashed into the lower part of his right leg, streaked up through the leg, and punched its way out of the body through the hip.

A surgeon later told Patton, "It was a miracle that the bullet didn't hit a bone or an artery. You would have been crippled or killed."

Angelo stopped the gushing blood with a piece of Patton's torn pants. Patton's face was contorted with pain, but he was still conscious. He told Angelo to get to the tanks and point out to them where the German machine guns were hidden. Angelo did so, and in the next hour the tanks destroyed 25 of the machine-gun nests. One nest kept firing even as the tank smashed into it. The two machine gunners were squashed to death. Over them the American tank men put up a sign: "To two brave men."

When the firing faded to a mutter, Patton was carried back to his command post, the pain so intense that he had

40

to clench his teeth to keep from screaming. At the command post he refused to be taken to a field hospital until he had written a report to his commanding general. He told the general how the tank corps had "stood its ground."

The next morning Patton wrote to Beatrice from his hospital bed. "I had seven captains, two majors and myself in the fight," he told her. "Of these all are hit but one captain and two majors . . . Captain English was killed and Captain Higgins got both eyes shot out. But the tank corps . . . only went forward. And they were the only troops in the attack of whom that can be said."

Patton was still recovering in the hospital when the war ended on November 11, 1918, his 33rd birthday. In the hospital he learned that he had been promoted to full colonel. And his general presented him with the DSC, the Distinguished Service Cross medal. Later Patton pinned another DSC onto the chest of Private Joe Angelo, who had saved his life and led the tanks to the German machine gunners.

In thinking about his walk into those machine-gun nests on that field at Cheppy, Patton realized he was no longer haunted by the demon that had nagged him since childhood. To his father he wrote, "I had always feared I was a coward at heart, but I am beginning to doubt it."

His courage now proven, Patton was still driven forward by the ambition he had revealed to his father and Beatrice long ago, his need to be hailed as great. "One day," he said, "I will make them all know me."

The day was coming, amid the thunder and flames of a second world war, when all the world would know him.

Battle for

Morocco

Patton stood on the deck of the cruiser *Augusta* as the big warship nosed out of the harbor at Norfolk, Virginia. Looking around him, Patton saw the masts of almost a hundred ships—battlewagons, cruisers, destroyers, troop ships, cargo ships.

They were streaming toward Africa, carrying the first American troops of World War II to leave for battle across the Atlantic. The troops were commanded by Major General George S. Patton.

Patton wrote in his diary, "When I think of the greatness of my job . . . I am amazed, but on reflection, who is as good as I am? I know of no one."

The years since World War I had been good ones for Patton. He and Beatrice raised two daughters and a son, who was now attending West Point. The Pattons were rich. Both he and Beatrice had inherited millions of dollars after the deaths of their parents. Patton bought and rode polo ponies. He sailed his yacht from California to Hawaii and back, guiding it through a storm in which he and Beatrice were lost in the vastness of the Pacific Ocean for almost a week.

A few years before the start of World War II, Patton had asked to be selected as the commander of the cadets at West Point. He wrote to a superior officer that he was one of the few officers still in the army who had fought on the battlegrounds of World War I. He could tell the cadets what war was really like. "I think," he wrote, "that a little blood and guts would be good for the cadets."

He also wrote to friends during the 1920s and 1930s about the future of tanks. He wrote to a friend and fellow tank officer, Dwight D. Eisenhower, "In the next war we will use them like cavalry. . . . We'll be able to smash through their front or around their flanks and hit them from the rear."

Maj. General Patton in tanker gear on the eve of World War II.

That prediction came true some 20 years later, in the summer of 1940. Another World War I veteran, German dictator Adolf Hitler, sent his tanks and armored cars through and around the French and British armies in Europe in a "blitzkrieg." Blitzkrieg means "lightning war" and like a flash of lightning, Hitler's tanks and troops blitzed through Poland, France, Belgium, Holland, Denmark, and Norway.

When the war began, Patton took command of an armored division that was training in the south. His flashy uniforms, which he designed himself, and his fighting speeches soon caught the attention of newspaper and magazine reporters. One writer learned about Patton's mention of "blood and guts." He gave Patton a nickname, "Blood and Guts," that would endure beyond Patton's lifetime.

In 1942, Hitler and his Japanese partners seemed to be winning World War II. The Nazi swastika flew across Europe—from France in the west to the frozen plains of Russia in the east, from near the Arctic Circle to Africa's Sahara Desert. Halfway around the world, Japan had wiped out American battleships in a surprise attack on Pearl Harbor. The Japanese captured General Douglas MacArthur's army in the Philippines. These were the two worst defeats in American military history.

But the Allies were fighting back. The Soviets had stopped Hitler's drive toward Moscow, their capital. And the Allies had decided on a strategy to squeeze Hitler to death.

First, the British and Americans would invade North Africa. The British would land in Algeria on the Mediterranean side. The Americans would land in Morocco on the Atlantic side. Between them they would trap Hitler's Afrika Korps. Then they would leap across the Mediterranean to the island of Sicily, and use Sicily as a stepping stone to Italy and France. From France they would push east toward Germany. The Soviets would be pushing from the west. Caught in the middle of this sandwich would be the Nazis. They would be crushed by the two onrushing armies.

Patton's old friend, Dwight D. Eisenhower, had risen swiftly in rank when America entered the war after Pearl

Patton, left, and an aide study maps during the 1941 war games.

Harbor. By 1942, Ike was the commanding general of the American, British, and Canadian armies in Europe. "You are my idea of a battle commander," Ike told Patton. He picked Patton to lead the American army in the invasion of Morocco.

Patton was delighted. But he was also worried. He feared his invading army would be thrown back into the Atlantic. At this time of the year, November, the coast of Morocco was pounded by huge waves. The small boats carrying soldiers to shore could be overturned by the churning surf. Even if the Americans got to the beach, they would be met by tough French troops. Morocco was then a colony of France. Would the French soldiers be loyal to their German conquerors and fight the Americans? They could slaughter the GIs who had never before faced the roaring guns of an enemy.

The outlook was "gloomy," Patton told Ike. But he added, "Rest assured that when we start for the beach we shall stay there either dead or alive, and if alive we shall not surrender." He told his commanders, "Grab the enemy by the nose and kick him in the pants."

As his ships edged closer to Africa, Patton sent a message to his troops, "During the first few days after you get ashore, you must work unceasingly, regardless of sleep, regardless of food. A pint of sweat will save a gallon of blood. The eyes of the world are watching us; the heart of America beats for us; God is with us. On our victory depends the freedom or slavery of the human race. We shall surely win."

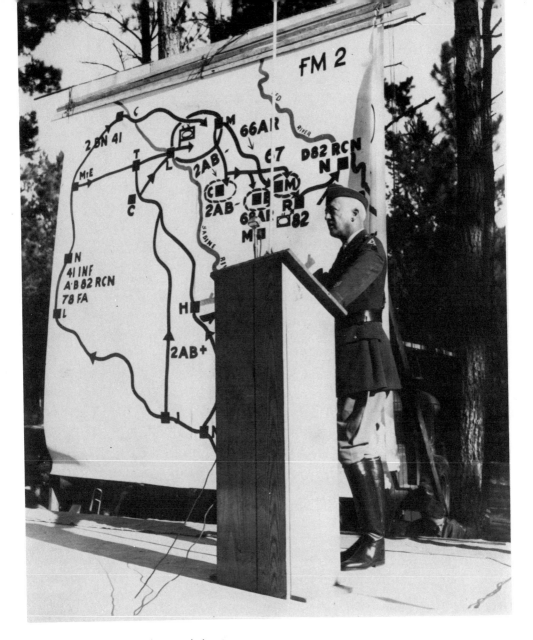

The commander explains
strategy to his troops.

Each day Patton paced the steel deck of the *Augusta*, peering toward a Morocco that lay beyond the horizon. He had changed since World War I. His hair was now silver. His 6-foot-1 body was still erect, but he had thickened around the middle.

Two days before the invasion a storm whipped the sea, tossing the ships like corks. Patton stood on the deck of the pitching *Augusta* and stared glumly at the huge, white-capped waves. His boats would be swamped. That night he slept fitfully.

He awoke the next morning, to stare unbelievingly through his porthole at a sea as flat as a table. He later wrote to his wife, "God was with us."

At five o'clock on the morning of November 8, Patton watched from the top deck of the *Augusta* as American warships began to bombard the shore. Tracer shells zipped through the darkness like angry red fireflies. He saw boats, filled with American GIs, stream toward the shore.

The sun rose, a red ball over the smoke and roar of guns. Patton ordered a boat to take him to the beach and the battle. A boat was swung from the side of the *Augusta*. Just then, the *Augusta's* guns roared at a French warship. Patton's boat was blown off its hooks. It flew into the sea, together with all of Patton's gear. Only minutes before, he had told an aide to take his pearl-handled pistol out of the boat. The pistol was the one that had shot Julio Cardenas at the Rubio Ranch some 25 years earlier.

That pistol was strapped to his side as Patton sloshed through the surf a few hours later. On the beach he was told that the Americans had captured a nearby town. They had a foothold on the African shore.

The next day, Patton stood on the beach bellowing at troops to unload supplies. French fighter planes zoomed over the beach, guns blazing. Bullets tattooed the sand around him, but Patton as usual stood erect as his men cowered behind boats.

Patton saw one soldier jibbering with fear. Patton kicked him. The GI straightened, ran back to a boat and began unloading it. "Some way to boost morale," Patton told his diary that night.

During the next few days Patton seemed to be everywhere—especially wherever someone was doing something wrong. "If you stopped during an advance," one of his commanders said later, "suddenly there he was coming down on you like the wrath of God." Even to another general Patton snapped, "If your troops don't move forward, don't *you* come back—except in a box."

His GIs, stung by his shouts, curses, and kicks, overwhelmed the French and surged toward Casablanca, the main city of Morocco. Four days after the landing, on November 11, 1942—Patton's 57th birthday—the French agreed to a cease-fire. Patton's army marched into Casablanca. The British, meanwhile, had landed in Algeria and seemed to have Hitler's armies trapped.

President Roosevelt chats with Patton in Casablanca
during a tour of the war zone by the President.

That winter of 1942–43 Patton lived in a palace in Casablanca. "I feel like a sultan," he told an aide. But he ached for combat. "I am a fighter," he wrote in his diary. "I wish I could go out and kill someone." He didn't have long to wait.

Death of a
Friend

A few months after Patton's victory in Morocco, Hitler's Afrika Korps attacked an American and British army in nearby Tunisia. The Germans routed the American II Corps at Kasserine Pass. Seeing monster-sized German Tiger tanks for the first time, Americans turned and ran. Hundreds were killed, wounded, or captured. British generals complained to Ike that the American soldiers "lacked the nerve to fight."

General Eisenhower put Patton in command of the 90,000 American GIs of the II Corps. Ike angrily told Patton to prove to the British that Americans could fight

Patton boards a plane to fly to Tunisia.
Note his ivory-handled pistol.

—and win. But as Patton turned to climb into a plane for the flight to Tunisia, Ike touched his old friend's arm and said to him, "I want you back as a commander, not as a casualty."

Patton had to grin. Twenty-four years earlier, on the battlefields of World War I, he had heard those same orders—and ignored them.

When he saw the soldiers of the American II Corps, Patton scowled. The men slouched when they walked, their posture a sign of their low morale. Defeat had made the enlisted men dislike themselves as well as their officers. Their faces were dirty and bearded, their uniforms wrinkled and stained.

Patton snapped out orders. "Soldiers who are old enough to shave will do so daily," he decreed. Neckties had to be worn even in combat. "It is absurd," Patton told his officers, "to believe that soldiers who cannot be made to wear the proper uniform can be induced to move forward in battle."

Patton's II Corps joined the British in an attack against the Afrika Korps' 200,000 Italian and German soldiers. Patton told one of his commanders: "Attack, and keep on attacking, even if you lose one-quarter of your men."

Later he wrote in his diary, "I feel quite brutal in issuing orders to take such losses, especially when I am personally safe, but it must be done. War can only be won by killing."

And he would not stay where he was personally safe. Each day he rode toward the front in his Jeep. As always, he wanted his GIs to see their general going forward.

One afternoon he stopped to talk to a colonel who had taken his insignia, an eagle, off his helmet. Patton asked him why he had removed the symbol of his rank.

"Because snipers shoot at officers," answered the colonel. "I cannot command if I am a casualty."

"You cannot command if the soldiers don't know you're a colonel," Patton retorted. The red-faced colonel pinned the eagle back onto his helmet.

Another day Patton came to a line of tanks stopped on a winding road. Patton angrily asked why they had stopped.

"There's a mine field on the road up ahead, General," a major answered.

"Mine fields don't do as much damage as people think," growled Patton. "Let's go."

"You're going to get killed, sir," the major said.

Patton's Jeep roared by the tanks. A second Jeep followed Patton, then the line of tanks. A mile down the road the second Jeep struck a mine. Patton waved the tanks on. They rolled into the next town, unharmed. Despite the casualties in the Jeep, Patton told the crews of the tanks, "We can't be stopped by our fears. Never take counsel of your fears."

One night, as Patton sat at his desk in his headquarters, Captain Dick Jenson, his aide, walked up to him and saluted smartly. Patton looked on young Jenson with the same fondness he had for his son, then a cadet at West Point. The Jenson and Patton families had been close friends in California for years. Dick was carrying a small, tightly furled flag. The young officer had been waiting almost a year for this moment. On the red flag were three white stars, the three stars of a lieutenant general. Ike had just promoted Patton.

That night Patton slept under the three-starred flag. "When I was a little boy at home," he later wrote in his diary, "I used to wear a wooden sword and say to myself, 'George S. Patton, Jr., Lieutenant General.' At that time I did not know there were full generals. Now I want, and will get, *four* stars."

Ike pins a third star on the new Lt. General Patton.

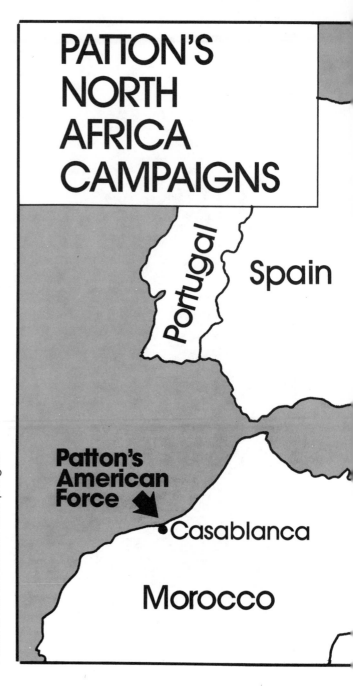

France

Italy

Mediterranean Sea

Sicily

British Force

Algeria

Tunisia

The Americans and the British drove back the Afrika Korps. British generals no longer claimed the American GI lacked nerve. But Patton was still not satisfied. One day an American division stormed a hill but fell back amid a hail of shells and bullets. Patton phoned the division's commanding general and told him, "You, personally, will lead a charge to take that hill." The general did lead the charge, and was wounded. But the Americans took the hill.

One day, as his Jeep bounced down a road, Patton and his driver heard the roar of a plane. They turned and saw a German fighter diving at them. The driver jammed on the brakes. He and Patton dove into a ditch. Bullets ripped up the ground around them as the plane zoomed a few feet above them, the engine's roar shaking the ground.

"I still get scared under fire," Patton confessed in a letter to his wife. "The strafing is the worst. I guess I will never get used to it, but I still poke along."

By April of 1943 the Afrika Korps had its back almost at the sea. Patton ordered one of his tank commanders to try to punch through the Nazi line, race to the sea, and surround the Korps. Staff officers were in short supply so Patton sent Captain Jenson to help out.

As the tanks attacked, German planes spotted the headquarters and roared over, dropping bombs. Jenson dived into a trench. A 500-pound bomb hit nearby and the concussion killed young Jenson instantly.

The body was brought back to Patton's headquarters for burial, wrapped in canvas. Patton knelt, rolled back the canvas, silently said a prayer, then kissed the forehead of the man he had loved like a son.

He wrote, "I can't see the reason that such fine young men get killed. I shall miss him. . . ." The cost of war hit Patton hard.

A few days afterwards he visited a field hospital and saw a soldier whose leg had been blown off. He asked how he was feeling and the soldier said, "Fine, since you came to see me."

"I suppose I do some good," he said later of his frequent visits to hospitals. "But it always makes me choke up. I have no personal feeling of responsibility for getting them hurt, as I took the same chances, but I hate to look at them."

Patton speaks to his troops.

The Afrika Korps was soon to surrender and Ike had a new job for Patton. He was to lead the American army in the invasion of Sicily, that island steppingstone to Italy.

Alongside the American army would be a British army, led by General Bernard "Monty" Montgomery. Patton disliked the British. He thought they were getting too much praise from Ike for the victory in North Africa. He promised himself that the British would not overshadow the Americans in Sicily. The Americans, he told himself, would get the praise they deserved. Not surprisingly, then, the battle for Sicily became a race between Patton and Montgomery, a race, Patton told his troops, "We must win."

The Race for
Messina

The first wave of Patton's Seventh Army landed on the Sicilian beaches on July 10, 1943. Writing on board the warship that carried him to Sicily, Patton told his diary, "I am leading 90,000 men in a desperate attack. . . . If I win, I can't be stopped. If I lose, I shall be dead."

He was very much alive as he ordered the driver of his Jeep toward the town of Gela. He could hear the thunder-like roar of artillery coming from the town. Two German divisions, led by Tiger tanks, had charged into Gela and were pushing American troops back toward the sea.

Shells lobbed by American battleships crashed into the streets of Gela. Fire and smoke erupted from smashed houses. Patton's Jeep screeched to a stop in front of the town's tallest building. Patton and his men ran up the stairs to the top. From there they could watch the battle for Gela. Patton saw a line of German soldiers advancing toward the town. He also saw that he and the other Americans inside the town were cut off from the American troops landing on the beaches. He sent a messenger with orders to an American division outside the town. The division was told to link up with the Americans inside Gela.

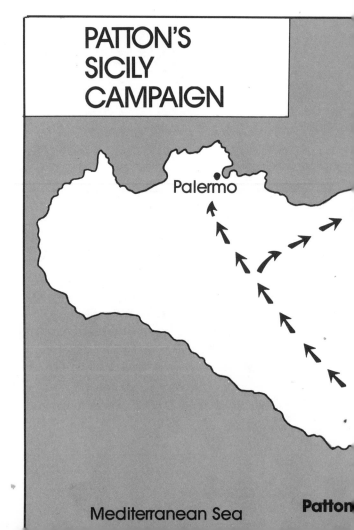

PATTON'S SICILY CAMPAIGN

Palermo

Mediterranean Sea

Patton

Two German planes zoomed low, dropping bombs. Two bombs hit the building that Patton was using as an observation post. The building shook but did not collapse.

Minutes later Patton was told that the division had linked up with the Americans inside Gela. He drove to where American infantrymen were battling the Germans outside the town. He joined a platoon of GIs, grabbed a mortar shell, dropped it into the barrel of a mortar, and watched the shell explode among German tanks and

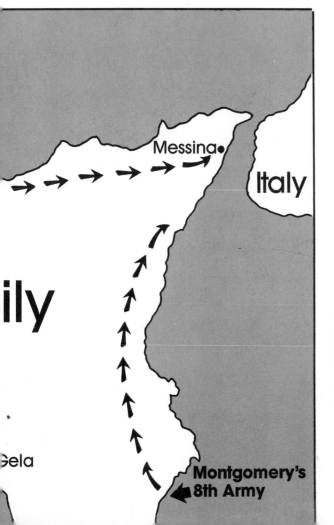

Patton's Sicily Campaign.

Patton comes ashore at Gela...

soldiers no more than a few football fields away. The mortar shells scattered the Germans and dozens rushed toward Patton's troops, hands held high in surrender.

An hour later he drove back to Gela on a road that ran between the two fighting armies. A sudden charge by the Germans would have netted America's most famous frontline general. Riding between the two armies, Patton noted in his diary that night, was "quite a lonesome feeling."

During the next few days, Patton's Seventh Army knifed north to capture the western half of the island. British General Bernard "Monty" Montgomery's Eighth Army also thrust north. Monty's most important task was to capture the port of Messina at the tip of the island. If Messina were taken quickly, hundreds of thousands of Nazi troops

...and watches his troops come ashore.

would be trapped on the island and forced to surrender. Glory would go to the army that took Messina—and Patton wanted that glory.

"This is a horse race," Patton told one of his commanders, "in which the prestige of the U.S. Army is at stake. We must take Messina before the British."

Patton's Seventh Army completed its capture of West Sicily in 12 days. His troops stood 150 miles west of Messina. Monty's Eighth Army was 100 miles south of the city. The frantic Germans and Italians were rushing toward Messina, hoping to escape by ship to Italy before they were trapped.

Patton ordered two of his commanders, Generals Omar Bradley and Lucian Truscott, to drive toward Messina. "Land your troops from the sea behind the German lines at night," he told the generals.

Both generals frowned. "Nighttime landings are too risky," Truscott told Patton.

"Be bold, be bold," Patton replied.

Truscott's soldiers did manage to sneak ashore in darkness. Now the Germans had Americans in front of them and behind them. They fled toward Messina. Patton chased them and his advance guard entered the town on the night of August 16, 1943.

The next morning, Patton and his staff zoomed toward Messina, shells bursting all around. One car directly behind Patton was struck by a fragment, its wheel knocked off. Another car was blown off the road, all of its occupants wounded.

Patton enters shell-torn Messina on the morning
of August 17, 1943.

Patton's Jeep bounded into Messina, untouched. Minutes later a lone tank rumbled into the town carrying a general sent by Monty to claim the town for the British. The general saw Patton standing triumphant in the center of the town, surrounded by grinning American GIs. The general saluted Patton and said, "It was a jolly good race, sir. I congratulate you."

Most of the German and Italian troops, however, had escaped to Italy. That country would be the next battleground of the war. But not for Patton. Suddenly it seemed that his fighting days were over.

During the drive to Sicily, Patton visited hospitals to cheer up the wounded. He saw one soldier dying, the top of his head cut off. He told himself to avoid looking at the dying. Seeing men die, he said, might build up "personal feelings about sending men into battle. That would be fatal for a general."

In one hospital he saw a soldier who was not wounded. Patton asked him why he was in the hospital.

"It's my nerves," sobbed the soldier. "I can't stand the shelling anymore." He went on crying uncontrollably.

"Your nerves, hell," Patton shouted. He called the man a coward.

The man couldn't stop crying. "Shut up!" Patton roared. "I won't have these brave men who have been shot at, seeing you. . . ." He swung his glove, slapping the soldier's face.

The news spread swiftly across Sicily. Patton had slapped a combat-weary soldier. Ike was furious. He ordered Patton to apologize to the soldier and to all the men and women of the Seventh Army.

Patton feared that Ike would send him home in disgrace. His days of war would be ended. He apologized to each of his divisions, standing in front of a microphone

Patton comforts wounded GIs during the battle for Sicily.

and offering his "sincere regret." Some of his troops did not believe Patton needed to apologize. And when he stood before Truscott's Third Division, a chant rose from the ranks: "No . . . No . . . General . . . No . . ."

The chant stopped. Again Patton tried to speak.

"No . . . No . . . General . . . No . . ."

Tears in his eyes, Patton turned from the microphone and strode away.

In America, angry parents and wives of Seventh Army soldiers demanded that Ike remove Patton from command. "It's up to you," Ike was told by his superiors in Washington. Ike pondered. Should he get rid of his best fighting general?

Breakout!

Ike decided to keep Patton. But he had warned him. One more ugly incident like the slapping and Patton would be fired. Patton had sighed with relief. Now he could go on fighting.

But on D-Day, June 6, 1944, when American, British, Canadian, and French troops invaded Europe at the Normandy beaches, Patton was still in England. General Omar Bradley, who had served under Patton, was now in charge of the American armies in France. "I hope they don't win the war without us," Patton wrote to his wife. "It is hell to be on the sidelines and see all the glory eluding us. . . ."

A month after the D-Day landings in Normandy, however, Allied troops had moved only 30 miles into France.

Patton's campaigns
in France and Germany.

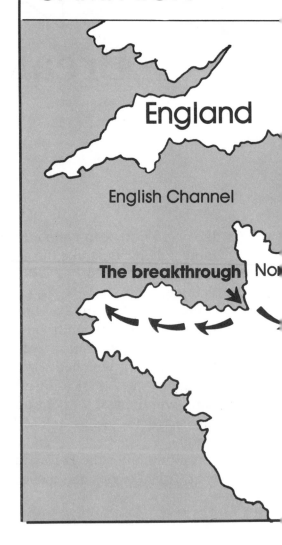

Berlin •

Neth.

Belgium

Bastogne •

The
Ardennes

Lux

Germany

Paris •

France

Switzerland

At a conference in France, Patton chats
with General Bradley (left) while Willie sleeps.

Patton was ordered into action, in charge of the Third Army, fresh from the U.S.

Now he stood before these men. He wore riding pants and a tight-fitting battle jacket, the ribbons on his chest a blaze of color. His boots glistened and his silver spurs flashed in the sunlight. He gripped a riding crop as he spoke.

"Death must not be feared," he told his troops. "Some men are cowards, yes, but they fight just the same. The real hero is the man who fights even though he's scared. Some men get over their fright in a minute under fire, others take an hour, for some it takes days. But the real man will never let the fear of death overpower his honor, his sense of duty. . . ."

That fiery speech had been hurled at his troops for months as Patton trained them for combat. "When he finished," one Third Army soldier later recalled, "you felt that here was a man you would go to hell and back for."

Trotting at Patton's side in Normandy was a dog named Willie. Willie had been the pet of a British pilot and had flown in bombing raids over Germany. When the pilot was killed, a British officer gave the dog to Patton. Tail wagging, Willie trailed after Patton for the rest of the war. When bombs exploded near Patton's headquarters, Willie dived under the table. "Willie," Patton wrote, "doesn't like to hear shells come that close any more than does his master."

Patton's first message to his troops was "Now . . . let's get the hell on to Berlin." And Blood and Guts promised that he personally would shoot Hitler "just like I would a snake."

First, however, the Allies had to fight their way out of Normandy. Ike decided on a plan, called Operation Cobra. Waves of bombers flew over the German troops near the town of St. Lo, dropping tons of bombs. The bombing was so heavy that five miles away, Allied soldiers clapped hands over their ears to shut out the deafening roar. The earth shook under their feet.

The bombs blew away tanks and guns. A huge hole was ripped in the German line. Through that hole Ike sent George Patton and the tanks of his Third Army. "I don't have to urge you to keep them fighting," Ike told Patton. "That is one thing I know you will do."

The Third Army broke out of Normandy and pursued the Germans over the hot and dusty plains of France. Patton rode in his Jeep only a few miles behind his tanks. Scolding, screaming, and cursing, he urged them on. One day his Jeep roared up to the headquarters of the Sixth Armored Division. The division's tanks had stopped at the edge of a river. "There are German guns on the other side of the river," an officer told Patton.

Patton demanded to see the division's commanding general. "Have you been down to the river?" he snapped at the general.

The general said he had not.

"Unless you do something," Patton growled, "you'll be out of a job."

Inside Gela, a rifleman at his side, Patton eyes a deserted street.

Patton drove to the river. He saw German soldiers on the other side, but their guns were silent. Patton ordered the tanks to cross the river, which was only a foot deep. That afternoon the division's tanks were again racing eastward toward Germany.

Patton's Jeep crosses the Seine. He was the first U.S. commander to cross that river in France.

That night he wrote to his wife, "I earned my pay today."

His Jeep bounced through the streets of towns liberated by his tanks only hours before. One morning he got too close to the tanks and was caught in a shower of shells. A sergeant, riding on the top of one tank, was blown to the ground, his arm hit by a splinter of steel. Rolling on the ground, the sergeant screamed, "I've lost my arm!"

"The hell you have, son," a voice said. The sergeant looked up and saw General George S. Patton bandaging the wounded arm.

Three weeks after breaking out of Normandy, the Allies freed Paris, the capital of France, and were sweeping toward Germany as fast as 60 miles a day. Patton's Third Army tanks led the way. A French general hailed Patton as "The Liberator of France."

But then the tanks stopped. They were out of gas. Patton radioed to Ike for more gas. Back came the word. They would have to wait.

Patton paced the floor of his headquarters, which was the back of a truck. He knew gas was going to other people, including French trucks which were bringing food into Paris. If he had that gas, he roared, "I could win this war."

Patton was right, German generals admitted after the war. The German army was shattered by Patton's lightning dash across France. "The gateway was wide open for Patton's tanks to roll into Germany," a German general wrote years later. "The war should have ended in August of 1944."

"The Liberator of France" with a happy Frenchman.

Instead, the war went on to the spring of 1945. The Germans were able to re-form their lines. And in December, 1944, Hitler unleashed the surprise attack that killed thousands of Americans in the Ardennes Forest. Only Patton's counterattack, saving Bastogne, prevented that defeat from becoming a disaster.

The Third Army hammered its way toward Germany. Patton demanded that his officers never give up an inch of ground that they had won. One day he was told that a division had retreated a few miles. Patton flew to the front and ordered two of the generals to the front. "Take the ground you gave up," he told the generals, "or don't come back."

Patton with one of his tanks during the breakout.

The generals regained the ground, but during the fighting one, Gen. Paul Baade, was wounded. The next day he wore the Bronze Star medal, pinned on his chest by Patton.

The Germans feared Patton more than any Allied general. Early in January of 1945 the German radio asked

Inside Germany, Patton mans a tank's gun.

warily, "Where will bloody Patton strike next?"

In mid-March he struck across the river Rhine, his tanks stabbing toward the heart of Germany. His Third Army was one of three Allied armies moving shoulder to shoulder toward Berlin. Approaching Berlin from the other side were the Soviets.

Allied troops smashed into Nazi concentration camps and looked with horror on the living skeletons of prisoners. These were the few left of the millions of Jews, and other peoples who had been tortured and killed during what is now known as the Holocaust.

Patton and Ike visited one camp. They saw "death rooms" in which prisoners had been gassed to death.

Ike, in cap, and Patton,
on his right, gaze with horror
at Holocaust victims.

They stared at gallows on which prisoners had been slow-ly strangled to death.

Patton ordered German civilians to walk through the camps to see the horrors of their Nazi masters. After visiting a camp, the mayor of one town went home and hanged himself.

An ex-prisoner shows Patton and Bradley, left, and Ike, right, a prison camp's gallows.

Patton rides a horse that Hitler had picked as a present to Emperor Hirohito of Japan.

Late in April 1945, Ike's army and the Soviet's came together in Austria like two giant hands clapping. Crushed between them were the remnants of Hitler's army. Hitler himself hid in a bunker in Berlin as Russian soldiers hunted him. Hitler shot himself. On May 8, 1945 the Germans surrendered. The war in Europe was over.

Patton pleaded to be sent to the Pacific to fight the Japanese. But there would be no more battles for George Patton.

Farewell to a
Fighter

It was a June day in 1945. Patton was back in the United States, and on his collar were the four stars of a full general, those stars he had wanted for so long.

He was in Boston, near where Beatrice had lived during the war. Hundreds of thousands of people cheered as he was driven in an open car through the streets. The parade ended at an outdoor theater where he spoke to an audience of 20,000 and the guests of honor, 300 wounded Third Army soldiers.

"These men are the heroes," Patton said in his piercing voice. Then he turned, drew himself erect, saluted the

Patton and his Third Army troops.

men below him, and walked back to his seat alongside Beatrice. The crowd stood and roared approval.

He and Beatrice flew to other tumultuous welcomes in California. They went to Washington where he visited a hospital filled with wounded Third Army soldiers. He saw a man who had lost both legs. Patton burst into tears and said, his voice shaking, "If I had been a better general, most of you wouldn't be here."

Back in Boston, he packed to return to Germany. His Third Army was occupying southern Germany. He said goodbye to his son, George S. Patton, Jr., soon to graduate from West Point and later to become a general himself. Alone with his two daughters, Patton said to them, "I won't be seeing you again."

"Don't be silly," one said. "The war is over."

"No," Patton said. "I have a feeling that my luck has run out at last."

Back in Germany, he was unhappy in peace. He

Captain George S. Patton III, the General's son, and his mother, shown here at the dedication of the new Patton 48 medium tank.

thought about quitting the army. "But what else is there?" he asked himself. Life had no meaning for Patton without the army, his life for over 35 years.

Ike had told Patton that one of his tasks was to make sure that no former Nazis had jobs in the new government. Patton didn't agree. If a former Nazi was doing a good job, he told American reporters, the Nazi should stay in office. His words infuriated people back in the United States, who had been horrified by Nazi brutalities. They demanded that Ike give Patton a new job.

Ike removed Patton and gave him command of a small army in Germany. Early in December, 1945, Patton decided to return to the U.S. to think over his future. He was now 60, one of the army's oldest generals. He thought about retiring to write his autobiography.

The day before he was to leave for home, Patton and a friend were driving in Patton's limousine. They were on their way to go hunting. As Patton's car sped down a narrow road, an army truck coming the other way veered into the limousine. The collision threw Patton forward. His head struck the ceiling of the car. His scalp was ripped open. When soldiers opened the car's doors, Patton told them he could not move his arms or legs. His spinal cord had been injured. At a hospital a doctor told Patton he would be paralyzed for life.

Patton calmly nodded. When his wife arrived from the United States, he seemed to improve. But one evening, Patton told a nurse that he was going to die.

And on the evening of December 23, as he slept, his heart stopped. The death he had dodged on a hundred stormy battlefields had struck him down in the silence of a hospital bed.

The last resting place
of a fighter.

A few days later he was buried among his Third Army
dead in a military cemetery at Hamm in Luxembourg, not
far from the French–German border. A stark white cross,
identical to the crosses marking most of the other graves,
is inscribed:

> George S. Patton
> General Third Army
> California Dec. 21 1945

The words that might have been written above the
grave of George "Blood and Guts" Patton were said by
one of his Third Army soldiers:

"He did not ask his men to fight *for* him, he asked them
to fight *with* him."

BIBLIOGRAPHY

For those readers who want to know more about General Patton, I recommend these books, which I found helpful in learning the story of a complex man.

The Patton Papers, Volumes I and II, by Martin Blumenson. These contain much material from Patton's letters and diaries.

Patton, a Study in Command, by Martin Essame. The general as a strategist and a commander.

The Last Days of Patton, by Ladislas Farago. The general as a peacetime commander in Germany after World War II.

War As I Knew It, by General George Patton. Essays written by Patton after World War I, and before, during and after World War II.

Portrait of Patton, by Harry Semmes. A look at the general by one of his close friends and aides.

When the Third Cracked Europe, by George J. B. Fisher. The Third Army racing across France into Germany.

Lucky Forward, by Robert S. Allen. A look at Patton and the Third Army by a former Third Army officer.

Patton: Ordeal and Triumph; by Ladislas Farago. The general in good times and bad times.

INDEX